Backyard Ecosystems

Henry Cassidy

Rosen Readers

Rosen Classroom™

New York

Published in 2014 by The Rosen Publishing Group, Inc.
29 East 21st Street, New York, NY 10010

Book Design: Mickey Harmon

Photo Credits: Cover S. Cooper Digital/Shutterstock.com; pp. 3, 4, 6, 8, 10, 12, 14, 16, 18, 20, 22–24 (clouds) Just2shutter/Shutterstock.com; p. 5 Hemera/Thinkstock.com; p. 9 tolmachevr/Shutterstock.com; p. 11 Ami Parikh/Shutterstock.com; p. 13 mchin/Shutterstock.com; pp. 15 (deer), 19 (fox) Pim Leijen/Shutterstock.com; p. 15 (caterpillar) Ali Mufti/Shutterstock.com; p. 15 (rabbit) Elena Sherengovskaya/Shutterstock.com; p. 17 Ekaterina Pokrovskaya/Shutterstock.com; p. 19 (mantis) jps/Shutterstock.com; p. 21 clearviewstock/Shutterstock.com; p. 22 (hummingbird) Birdiegal/Shutterstock.com.

ISBN: 978-1-4777-2551-1
6-pack ISBN: 978-1-4777-2552-8

Manufactured in the United States of America

CPSIA Compliance Information: Batch #CS13RC: For further information contact Rosen Publishing, New York, New York at 1-800-237-9932.

Contents

Backyard Fun

You may spend a lot of time in your backyard. Although you use it as a place to hang out, your backyard is home to many living creatures. What lives there? Your backyard may be **overflowing** with plants, animals, and creepy-crawly critters.

All backyards are different because people live in different **environments**. Your backyard may have different plants and animals than your friend's. However, every creature in any backyard is always part of an ecosystem. Learning about ecosystems is helpful in understanding the natural world that surrounds us.

Backyards bring people a lot of enjoyment, but are also good homes for plants and animals.

An ecosystem is a group of plants and animals that need each other to stay alive. Each part of an ecosystem is equally important. That means every plant and animal has a job to do. Some provide food or homes to other creatures in the ecosystem. Others make the soil healthy. These are only a few examples.

No matter what its job is, each living creature is needed to keep an ecosystem healthy. If one part is taken away, or something is put there that doesn't belong, it can hurt the whole ecosystem.

Can you see how each part of an ecosystem coexists, or gets along, in this backyard?

Busy Backyard Ecosystem

What's a Habitat?

Backyards have ecosystems because they're habitats. A habitat is the natural place where a plant or animal lives. There can be countless ecosystems in one habitat.

So, why do plants and animals live in backyards? Backyards provide all the **resources** they need to survive. Creatures in other habitats may need different kinds of resources, so they can't live in backyards. That's why a backyard ecosystem has different creatures than other ecosystems, such as an ocean or jungle.

Chipmunks make their homes in backyards. Most backyards have enough food, sunlight, and water for chipmunks to stay alive.

Food Chains

All habitats have connections between plants and animals called food chains. Food chains show us what eats what in a habitat. Every plant, bug, and animal is one step in the chain. This is why each creature is needed to keep the whole habitat healthy.

If a certain plant or animal were missing, the ecosystem would be unbalanced. This would cause some creatures to die. As long as there are enough resources to support each part of the food chain, the ecosystem can stay strong.

Without these plants, many animals and bugs wouldn't have food!

Pretty Plants

Strong ecosystems start with strong plants. They're the first step in a food chain because they don't eat anything. They make their own food using sunlight. Because they make their own food, they're called producers.

What kinds of plants are in a backyard? Backyards usually have trees, grass, and flowers. If you have a vegetable garden in your backyard, that's part of the ecosystem, too. The plants in an ecosystem **attract** animals that use them as food.

Grasshoppers live in backyards
that have the food they need to survive.

Animals in an Ecosystem

Animals that eat, or consume, plants are the next step in a food chain. They're called consumers since they can't make their own food. These plant-eating animals are also called herbivores (UHR-buh-vohrz). That means they don't eat meat. There are plenty of plants in backyards, so it's a great place for herbivores to find food!

There are many kinds of backyard herbivores. Caterpillars eat leaves on trees. Butterflies feed on flowers. Rabbits eat leafy plants and grass. If you live near woods, deer may visit your backyard, too.

Backyard plants give all these animals food. Without plants, the ecosystem wouldn't exist.

Animals aren't just part of a food chain. They do a very important job when they come to backyards. They help new plants grow.

Animals and bugs help ecosystems by spreading plants' seeds or pollen to other places. For example, a squirrel may eat an apple from a tree in your backyard. When it finishes, it may carry a seed to another backyard. This seed may grow into a new tree, which will play an important role in that backyard's ecosystem. Can you see how important this job is?

Squirrels are a big part of a backyard's ecosystem. They eat plants, but help spread seeds to grow new plants, too.

Top of the Food Chain

If the herbivores in a backyard went **unchecked**, they would eat all the plants. The next step in the food chain controls this. They're called carnivores (KAHR-nuh-vohrz). Carnivores are consumers that eat only meat.

One of the most feared backyard predators is the fox! Foxes find a lot of yummy food in backyards, such as rabbits and birds. Foxes must be quick and quiet in order to catch their prey. Some bugs are carnivores, too. Praying mantises eat grasshoppers and other bugs. Sometimes, they eat other praying mantises!

Carnivores are at the top of the food chain. They control the number of critters, which helps keep the ecosystem balanced.

One Last Step

There's one last part of an ecosystem's food chain. It's the decomposers (dee-kuhm-POH-zuhrz). They're just as important as the steps before them. Decomposers are creatures such as bugs and worms. You may have seen some in your backyard, but do you know what they do?

Decomposers put **nutrients** into the soil by breaking down dead plant and animal matter. Healthy soil allows plants to grow strong. This is very important, since plants support the rest of the ecosystem.

Decomposers may seem icky, but they're really important!

Nature at Work

Backyards are busy habitats, bursting with wildlife that make up interesting ecosystems. Spending time in your backyard is a fun way to see nature at work. If you see squirrels running from tree to tree or a bird with a worm in its mouth, you'll know why!

Backyard ecosystems may have different plants and animals based on where you live. Desert areas could have cacti and snakes, while backyards with water could have lily pads and turtles. What lives in your backyard?

Glossary

attract (uh-TRAKT) To draw or pull toward.

environment (ihn-VY-ruhn-muhnt) Everything in the world that surrounds a living thing.

nutrient (NOO-tree-uhnt) Something plants and animals need to survive.

overflow (oh-vuhr-FLOH) To have more than what is needed.

resource (REE-sohrs) Something found in nature that can be used to survive.

unchecked (uhn-CHEHKD) Not controlled.

Index